The World is not Ready for You

KEVIN MCLEMORE

RMK PRODUCTIONS PUBLISHING

Introduction

You have something special; you have greatness in you. Many people talk about the law of attraction or the secret to success. I don't believe that there's a secret to success. I believe that there's a *system* to success and that is what my very good friend, Kevin McLemore, has done.

Kevin has designed a blueprint that allows you to create a process that allows you to fill in the blanks to lead you to a place *within* yourself that you can't go *by* yourself, so that you can do three main things that are so very important today.

One: Build your faith to fortify your level of perseverance and expand your level of self-awareness mentally, emotionally, and spiritually.

Two: Give you the tools to navigate this new disruptive area where we are. In this process, you're not only reflecting and being given some tools that allow you to begin to put a gameplan together to move your life in the direction of where you want to go, but it will also help you to live a life that will outlive you by getting clarity about the mark and the impact and the legacy that you want to leave.

Three: Show you how to build a community of collaborative, achievement-driven, supportive relationships. We can't do this thing called life by ourselves. This book, I feel, is very strong in bringing people together.

As we begin to change how we see ourselves, we will change the world that we live in, and be able to impact generations yet on-going.

To Your Greatness,
Les Brown
The World's #1 Motivational Speaker / Trainer

Forward

While having the privilege of serving as Kevin McLemore's entertainment lawyer, I have come to know a man with many gifts. He is a dynamic speaker, health and wellness coach, podcast host, author, influencer, successful entrepreneur, and dedicated family man. Though humble, his circle of influence is vast. His social and professional circles are filled with dignitaries, thought leaders and celebrities. So, when asked to write this forward, I was as confused as I was honored. "You're an award-winning author and I'm a newbie who's taken 4 years to "almost be done" with my first book!", I said. **Kevin's response was "don't undersell your gift".** With that, I opened the book and dove in.

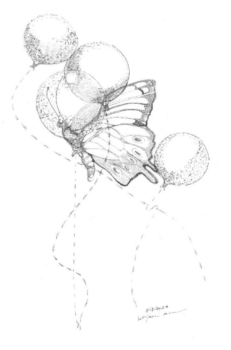

Page by page as I was drawn in deeper, it all made sense. I thought back to our many emails, texts, and conversations. Kevin finds a place in every exchange to impart wisdom and encourage. I leave a better person than I came even when I'm supposed to be providing the advice! But that's exactly who Kevin McLemore is, to his core. It's in his DNA to see the best in others and then to turn the mirror on them so they can see it too.

With *The World Is Not Ready For You*, Kevin McLemore shares with us his uncle Bill's prophetic words and the profound impact they have had on his life. From a foundation of just seven words, Kevin himself became the cornerstone from which an entire framework of inspirational work and impactful messages would be built. We all understand the importance of a solid foundation. Think about a house for example. Not only does it hold a house above ground, but it also serves protective purposes such as keeping out moisture, resisting movement of the ground around it and insulating from the cold. An inadequate foundation will crack, leak and even allow for infestation. A proper foundation provides security and lasts forever.

Uncle Bill (and other beautiful souls who touched Kevin's life like his grandparents) laid a foundation for his life that not only made him feel loved and supported, but also gave him the strength to persevere through life's trials and tribulations. Like all of us, he has been in and out of love, won and lost, been on top of the world and looked up from the bottom. But because he was told at a young age that he was so ordained for greatness, the world was not ready for him, Kevin had the courage to believe that he "could". He was resistant to cracking under pressure, sinking in defeat, or letting negativity infest his spirit. Rather, he went on to achieve greatness educationally, professionally and through his personal growth and development.

And perhaps most importantly, Kevin didn't just accept the pearls of wisdom for his own benefit. Instead, Kevin has built an entire world dedicated to uplifting people with the kinds of words and examples that were bestowed upon him. From the health and wellness training he has provided clients over the years, to the wisdom imparted through his award-winning books, Kevin shares the gifts he was given at every turn. Even his podcasts were created to inspire, motivate, and effectuate change. Through the stories of others, Kevin "shows" people better than HE can tell them.

The World Is Not Ready For You shows a side of Kevin that speaks to the most vulnerable places in us all. He expands Uncle Bill's seven powerful words, not with verboseness, but with the beauty of bold simplicity. Like Haikus, Chinese proverbs or Biblical scriptures, Kevin builds a few phrases around the mantra that add emphasis and perspective which provides a personalized serving of food for thought for the reader.

You will never forget his Uncle Bill's life changing words. *For the first time ever*, Kevin reveals his beautiful artwork! An homage to his beloved sister Brandy, each illustration incorporates a butterfly which makes them as symbolic as they are beautiful. Butterflies are a metaphor for hope, love, endurance, transformation, and rebirth. Kevin's butterflies draw us to each page like a place you want to visit again and again. And with each return, whether you ponder his words or admire his drawings, you will gain a deeper understanding of your own potential and ability to achieve anything if you step into your power.

In keeping with the messaging and goals of the book, Kevin calls you to action by providing opportunities throughout to put your thoughts into action. Carefully curated prompts lead you to share your thoughts, personal experiences and interpretations of the lessons. You are able to write on the dedicated journal pages so that you are no longer a passive reader, but rather an active participant led through a journey of growth and transformation.

The fact is, Kevin could have had anyone write this forward. But he chose me. And I'm grateful. I just hope that while Kevin gets the world ready for me and you, that I have likewise prepared each of you for the rebirth of Kevin McLemore: a man standing atop his strong foundation of legacy, bearing his soul for the betterment of others, laser focused and with a mission to educate, inspire and motivate you to step into your greatness. "Get ready world! This is Kevin McLemore at his best!"

- Heather Beverly
Entertainment Attorney, Speaker & Author of *Soul Reciprocity*

Preface

My uncle has repeatedly told me that he has to get the world ready for me because, for reasons unbeknownst to me, I have been called to do something special in this world to impact humanity. None of us are with a shero or hero in our life; for those of us who have been blessed with someone who gives without thoughts of him or herself, this is God's blessing by placing a hero in your life. That person is the anchor on which you can build a foundation to land your hopes and dreams.

My baby sister, Brandy McLemore, was that person for me.

She died at the age of forty-two.

I got the call on December 15, 2022, from my elder brother, Mack, and to say it impacted my world is an understatement. Brandy is—was…

Through my podcast, "Talking *wit* Kevin and Son," I have been showcasing people you should know—everyday people with stories that would otherwise have gone untold.

Today, each of us is the best version of who we are *right now*. We are all unique in our own way, by design.

Where you are right now is where you need to be. It may not be where you want to be, but it is where you *need* to be—until the day comes when you get to where you *want* to be. Moments matter, and if God grants us another day, don't make Him regret it. Today is the day you get a second chance to get things right because tomorrow is not promised to any of us.

When you read this story, you will believe that I am speaking directly to you—because I am. Do the difficult things while they are easy and great things while they are small. Your life today is designed by you; if you want today to be better than yesterday, design a better today and go from whatever happened to you yesterday and move forward. We are all unique, we are all special, and we all have the gift of greatness within ourselves. The world is not ready for you, so I just might have to get the world ready for you.

Dedication

I dedicate this book to champions who champion young champions. To those who give of themselves with no regard of the return. For those who see endless potential in someone else and map out a course for them to follow.

This book is dedicated to future leaders—young women and men who live beyond *I think I can* to get things done.

I dedicate this to the person who gave this book to you, because he or she can see all the places *you* will go—because, before *you* saw the potential in you, someone else saw your gift and had to get the world ready for you.

This is my gift to all the mentors, coaches, believers, and young starters, because… I believe in *you*.

The Gifter Of This Book Means to Me:

_____

_____

_____

_____

_____

_____

_____

When you look in the mirror, do you see what I see?
You have greatness within you.

I've got to get the world ready for you.

My Greatness:

_____

_____

_____

_____

_____

_____

_____

Your gift is your life;

today, be the best version of the person
you want your children to see.

I've got to get the world ready for you.

My Children Should See:

_____

_____

_____

_____

_____

_____

You have greatness within you
so there is magic in everything you do.

Maybe you will go places
you've never dreamt
of going before,

or maybe
you will do something
you've never done before.

I've got to get the world ready for you.

My Magic:

_____

_____

_____

_____

_____

_____

_____

Look at you and know that *you* are a blessing.

You can reach beyond the treetops
and place your dreams
on the tallest of buildings.

*I've got to get the world
ready for you.*

My Dreams:

_____

_____

_____

_____

_____

_____

_____

Never be ashamed of who you are,
be it tall or short, thin or wide,
light or dark.

Try everything.
Your life is your life;
the possibilities are endless.

Everything begins
and ends with you.

There is so much to this life for you to see
and do,

so do as much as you can.

I've got to get the world ready for you.

9

Who I Am:

_____

_____

_____

_____

_____

_____

_____

Don't just take selfies—journal,
keep your words close to your heart.

Your story will go where you go.

What you discover today will be a story
    never forgotten.

Take note, make notes.

Each new day gives you a second chance
                    to get *today* right.

I've got to get the world ready for you.

My Notes:

_____

_____

_____

_____

_____

_____

_____

Think of the magic you have—the power in your words.

Maybe *you* will be the person
    who will help others.

Maybe *you* will be the person
    who will impact the world
        and bring people together.

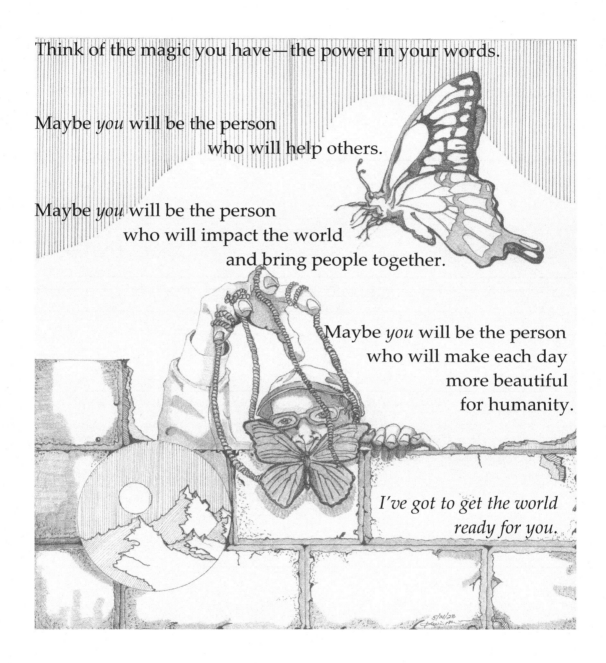

Maybe *you* will be the person
    who will make each day
        more beautiful
            for humanity.

*I've got to get the world
    ready for you.*

My Power:

_____

_____

_____

_____

_____

_____

_____

Or…

maybe you will do something so great
that people will stand in line for hours
and pay to hear your story.

I've got to get the world ready for you.

My Story:

_____

_____

_____

_____

_____

_____

_____

Look at your feet and place the right before the left.
Repeat again and again until each step leads you
to the things and places you love the best.

Let your heart lead you… see where it takes you.

I've got to get the world ready for you.

First Steps:

_____

_____

_____

_____

_____

_____

_____

Maybe *you* will be the one who will
speak up for those who will not
—or cannot—
speak for themselves.

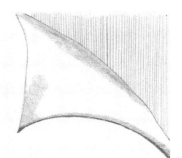

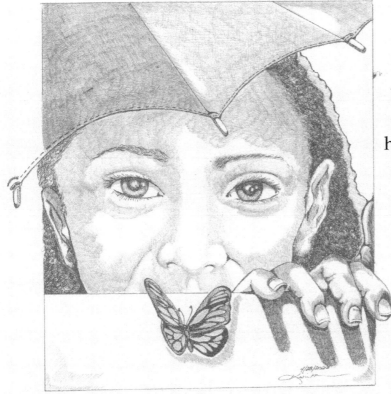

Love is love,
no matter
how it comes
packaged.

I've got to get the world ready for you.

Who I Speak For:

_____

_____

_____

_____

_____

_____

_____

Today is yesterday's *tomorrow*.
Where you are right now
is the only *you* there has ever been
— or will ever be.
Be smart and don't let the best part of you down.
Moments matter.

I've got to get the world ready for you.

Where I Am Right Now:

_____

_____

_____

_____

_____

_____

_____

Be patient—don't be in a rush to discover your *Why* because, in each phase of your life, your *Why* will be redefined until it and your purpose become aligned. Only then you will understand your *Why*.

I've got to get the world ready for you.

My Why Right Now:

_____

_____

_____

_____

_____

_____

_____

Life is not easy or fair.

There will be times when you will struggle.

There will be times when those closest to you
will let you down or betray you.

There will be times
when you might not want to go on.

Keep true to your faith and trust your gut.

Fear is what holds lesser men and women back, but not *you*.

Nothing worth having or being will come easy,
but *you* have greatness within you.

I've got to get the world ready for you.

My Fears:

_____

_____

_____

_____

_____

_____

_____

You *will* mess up some things.
You *will* make things harder for yourself without cause.

You may fall or
get knocked down,
but *you* have the
power to always get
back up.

Get knocked
down—get back up.
And *keep* getting back up
until the day no *one* or no *thing* will knock you down
ever again.

I've got to get the world ready for you.

27

When I Got Back Up:

_____

_____

_____

_____

_____

_____

_____

Can Do has nothing to do with Won't Do.

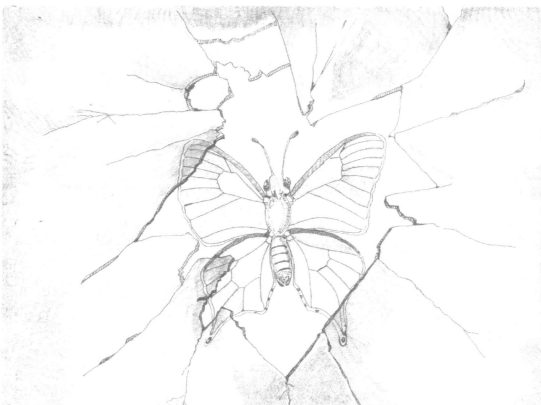

Can't and Can are the same thing if you believe them to be.
Where you are right now may not be where you want to be,
but you are where you are now for a reason.
You are only scratching the surface of what you can do
and who you will be.
The only person standing in your way of where *you* want to be
and who you will become is... *you.*

I've got to get the world ready for you.

What I Can Do:

_____

_____

_____

_____

_____

_____

_____

Take a good look into your mirror—excuses only sound good to the person making them. You have talent yet to be discovered; you have something wonderful inside you; you have the power to change the hearts of mankind.

You are something special.

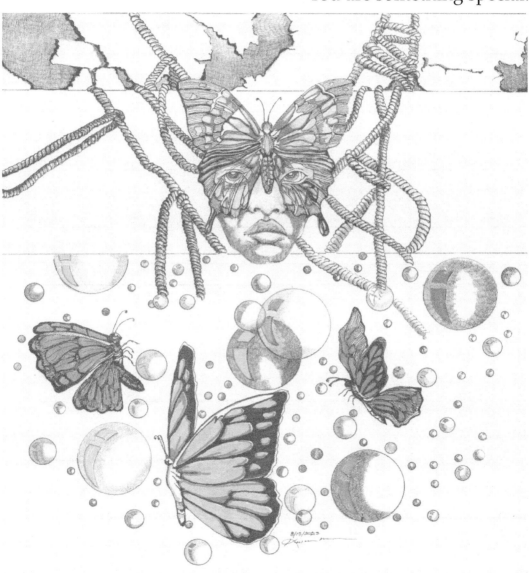

I've got to get the world ready for you.

My Talents:

_____

_____

_____

_____

_____

_____

_____

This moment is where your story begins—
with all the magical,
undiscovered potential you
hold inside.

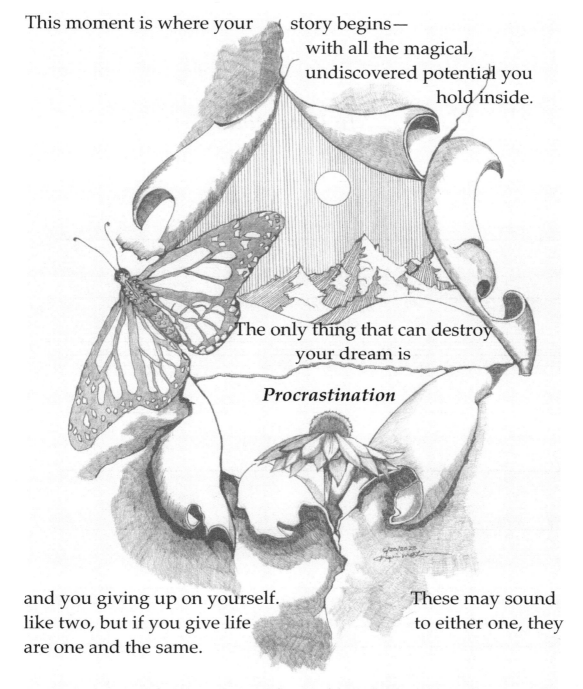

The only thing that can destroy
your dream is

Procrastination

and you giving up on yourself. These may sound
like two, but if you give life to either one, they
are one and the same.

I have got to get the world ready for you.

My Potential:

_____

_____

_____

_____

_____

_____

_____

Wherever you go, always take *Hope* with you.
Help other people every day.
 Pack as many cases of dreams
        as you can imagine.

Position key people in
 your life who will
celebrate your successes…
and embrace your failures.

The key to making dreams
come true is to always surround
yourself with people
who want you to be
successful.

Position yourself so
that you are doing the
work every day so those
around you will be
successful as well.

The company you keep will either help to build a better life or
destroy the life you are trying to build.

You have greatness with you.

I've got to get the world ready for you.

My Key People:

_____

_____

_____

_____

_____

_____

_____

A bird learns to fly after it's been pushed out of the nest;
education is part of the foundation of all progress and growth.

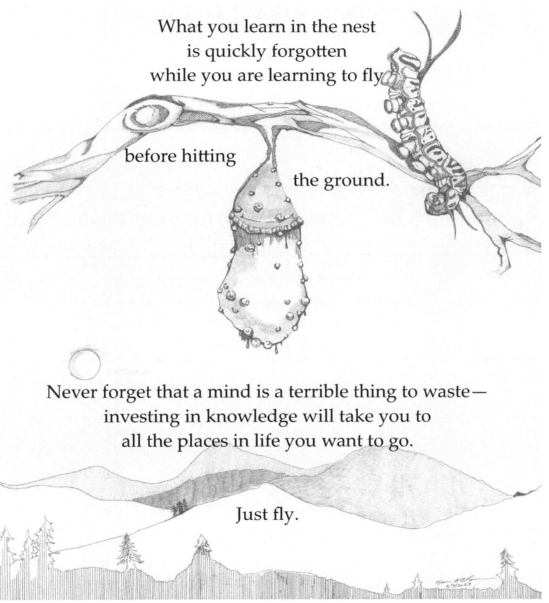

What you learn in the nest
is quickly forgotten
while you are learning to fly

before hitting

the ground.

Never forget that a mind is a terrible thing to waste—
investing in knowledge will take you to
all the places in life you want to go.

Just fly.

I've got to get the world ready for you.

Where I Want To Go:

_____

_____

_____

_____

_____

_____

_____

See yourself where you'd like to be—maybe speaking in front of a cheering crowd or wiping away a tear from the cheek of someone you love. Maybe you'll be the one who will shine a light into someone's heart who refuses to see. And, just maybe, you'll be that person they'll never forget, who will help them remember that, through the toughest of times, every winter brings a spring.

Don't ever give up because…

I've got to get the world ready for you.

My Tough Times:

_____

_____

_____

_____

_____

_____

_____

Because you are you, never lower yourself to hate;
do everything with love.
Trust your gut and follow your heart—
the exciting part is seeing where living with love will lead you.

I've got to get the world ready for you.

How I Live With Love:

_____

_____

_____

_____

_____

_____

_____

I got to get the world ready for you
because the world's *not* ready for you.
You have greatness within you,
and you are ready to do big things…
special things.

Could you be the one?

Life is about chance and choice,
and the actions that follow each.

Because I care, I share.

I've got to get the world ready for you.

My Choices and Actions:

Maybe, right now, you may not be in a place to know just how good you can be, but what does matter is right now and accepting the fact that you know that who you *are* really matters.

But change the way you have been feeling about yourself to where you can feel how special you are.

Keep in mind that, while you are trying to figure everything out, the world has been waiting for someone exactly like you, and it's my job to get the world ready, because, right now, the world is not ready for someone as special as *you*.

I've got to get the world ready for you.

I Am Special Because:

_____

_____

_____

_____

_____

_____

_____

Today is yesterday's tomorrow. Time and death are the two things no one can escape. There are 86,400 seconds in a day, 186 hours in a week, 52 weeks in a year; ask yourself what's more important, and what you're planning to do tomorrow. What if tomorrow never comes?

Whatever happened to you yesterday or what you did not get around to doing yesterday does not matter. Life happens in seconds; tomorrow is the future, so it does not exist; yesterday is history, so whatever you did or didn't do can't be done, edited, or changed. It is right now that matters, and because you have greatness within you…

I've got to get the world ready for you.

My Future:

_____

_____

_____

_____

_____

_____

_____

I've got to get the world ready for you.

My Disclaimer:

No one can make sense of this life, but to get anything done, life requires understanding, compassion, and action. Each person on this planet is a miracle, a gift to the human race; understanding what a real miracle is means you have to face the truth. The gift is to bring a healthy child into this world and teach them acceptance, with no limits or excuses attached to their subconscious; to allow them to fall down and to get back to their feet on their own; to take away the excuse that they hate to read, hate people without cause, but to find a book that they love reading, and be close enough with their faith that they are open to being loved and giving love. Allow them to become whoever or whatever they want to be, on their timeline. Allow them to live a life without a public branding or label of who everyone else thinks they should be. Like a butterfly, the greatest gift that can be given to this world is a child who is free to live free. That is a miracle, because we all have greatness within us. Each one.

That is why I have to get the world ready for you; the world is not ready for you.

The world is not ready for someone who is as special as you.

Special Thanks:

When I first put pen to paper for this book, I had spent three sleepless nights looking at the one picture of my baby sister sitting on my lap. Each word on the pages of this book was written behind a tear. For me, this has to be one of the greatest books I have ever written and I hope when people share their stories that this book will be part of their journey as they enter the next chapter of their life, because no one can do this one thing we call life alone. To Judi Fennell—a good friend, a world-class editor and a creative—I say thank you and I am so grateful for you, because you truly have greatness within you.

About The Author:

P. Kevin McLemore is a humble man of great passion and zest for life, who has devoted a lifetime to motivating people and pursuing and achieving everything he has set out to accomplish. Being raised by his grandparents, he learned the most important traits about human emotions, about being kind, having character, setting big goals, and chasing down your dreams like you stole them and were getting away.

His father always said that, out of all his kids, Kevin would run to the edge of a cliff and while all his sister brothers were looking over the edge to see how far it was to fall, Kevin would just jump, knowing he would always land on his feet. Dad was right; that's Kevin to a T. He believes in trying something new and that anything is possible, which is why his career and personal life reflect this positive, risk-taking attitude.

Kevin has never wavered in his resolution to set audacious goals and, not always but most of the time, has been successful. He has professionally gained the reputation of being one of the best fitness professionals and lifestyle coaches in the business, which is the reason he took on a project such as this one.

Kevin is President of RMK Production and the 10 United Podcast network, Co-host "Talking "wit" Kevin and son" the podcast, he also has made amazing accomplishments as a strength and endurance coach, track and field coach, athlete, marketing specialist, QVC pitchman, and master level fitness professional, coached IRONMAN athletes as well as three squash world champions. He has a lifelong passion to work with various youth groups and be a television spokesperson. Kevin became a first-time author with the *Letters to Elvis*. He has recently finished his third book *The Indispensable Game Of X's and O's; How I Learned Everything I'd Ever Needed To Know About Life By Playing High School Football, 57 And I Can, The Truth About Health and Fitness,* and *Dating With A Full Deck.* He intends to produce an animated Christmas story from his award-winning book, "Distinguished Authors Guild Award" Sprinkles, The True Spirit Of Christmas, which is another extension of how he wants to continue to help improve other people's lives.

More by Kevin McLemore

Dating with a Full Deck

KEVIN MCLEMORE

Chapter One

How Does Dating With A Full Deck *Work?*

It's Friday night, you're out at the bar. Across the room, you spot a sexy stranger. You feel the connection between the two of you. Something compels you to approach and introduce yourself. When you do, you strike up an immediate and easy conversation. You arrange a date. Within a few weeks, you've entered a relationship. Sound like a familiar scenario? Not likely. These days, in the world of swiping left and right, it's difficult navigating the world as a single person.

You might stumble upon someone whose outward appearance draws you in, or whose personality you think is wonderful, but it can feel impossible to take that long walk across the room to approach a total stranger or to take the mental and emotional leap of telling a platonic friend you're interested in more.

Consider *Dating With A Full Deck* as your own personal wingman, woman, or person. In this book, I'll provide you with a useful set of tools you can use to enter a meaningful dialogue with someone you know or someone you don't.

This book has nothing to do with any standard card game, but it comes with a deck of fifty-four cards that will make dating fun, engaging, and honest. Each card contains a question which, after you shuffle the deck and pull a card at random, you present that question to the person you're with (or the one you want to be with).

Early dating should be about having a good time while getting to know someone and having them get to know you. By allowing you to talk openly about what you're willing or not willing to do, what subjects or topics you are open to talking about, and those you'd rather not discuss, *Dating With A Full Deck* eliminates awkward silences, boredom, and even unintentional overshares.

There is no such thing as a perfect person or a perfect date yet being open from the outset will set you up to discover whether or not you have found someone who brings out the best in you and vice versa. Each chapter provides various insights about dating, love, and the early stages of a new relationship, and each card acts as a conversation springboard.

The book works especially well if both parties have read it prior to a first date, but that's not necessary. As long as one party has read the book and looked at the accompanying cards, you'll have all the ingredients for a great first date. Who knows? Start *Dating With A Full Deck* and your next first date just might end up being your last first date.

I remember the day of my first date. It was our big family trip for the summer at Kings Island, an amusement park in Mason, Ohio. It started out blazing hot. I was dressed in shorts and what is now called a muscle shirt (a tight t-shirt). It was midafternoon when, suddenly, the sky opened. We were near the Ferris wheel and the area was packed. My brother and I sought shelter under one of the game canopies. I had a towel with me to dry the sweat off my body. Out of nowhere, this beautiful mocha queen dashed under the canopy right next to me, soaked. My heart skipped a beat. I'm not sure if I had any game about me then, but without asking permission and without a formal introduction, I took my unused towel and placed it over her shoulders to dry her off. I didn't give any thought as to what could happen if she took offense at my random act of kindness and kicked me in the balls. I placed my towel over her shoulder, not knowing if I was risking my life or would get arrested for touching a stranger. My intentions were good. It turned out to be one of the best days of my life, my first kiss and relationship that would last for years and see the birth of my first child eight years later. This was truly dating with a full deck raw.

THE INDISPENSABLE GAME OF X'S AND O'S:

EVERYTHING I'D EVER NEEDED TO KNOW ABOUT LIFE,
I LEARNED BY PLAYING HIGH SCHOOL FOOTBALL

P.K. MCLEMORE

CHAPTER 1
HOW IT ALL GOT STARTED

When I began to keep a daily journal, Elvis was on his comeback tour and Richard Nixon was our nation's 37th President. I, on the other hand, was nothing but a young punk standing at one of the many crossroads in my life with my middle finger high in the air, intent on proving to all who doubted me that I didn't care what any of them thought. I wasn't going to continue to be controlled by my environment. I was going to take control of it.

When I was growing up, I thought I was the only one who had my set of problems. In fact, my story wasn't that different from the guy's next door. My parents divorced when I was in the third grade. My mother packed her bags and headed west to Beverly Hills 90210. My father got custody of my brothers, my sisters and me. Not long after the ink on the separation agreement dried, my dad moved us into his parents' home. It was my grandparents who acted as my parental role models. They taught me the fundamentals of a day's work for a day's pay, which I now call trading hours for dollars. And they offered love in the form of philosophical musings, practical advice, and supporting our basic needs, while my dad was busy drinking.

Like so many young African American men, I was raised in what society once called a "broken home" and now refers to as a "dysfunctional environment." To me, it didn't matter how anyone described what was happening in my house. What mattered to me was finding an answer to the question "What did I do to make my parents stop loving each other?"

I didn't understand that my mother and father were ill-equipped for love. I thought I wasn't lovable enough. I didn't have the right clothes, live in the right neighborhood, or go to the right school. Daily, I encountered those who, instead of referring to me as Kevin, Kev, or even K, called me "Boy" or used an even more pejorative word, which I will not repeat but which starts with an N and with which I am all too familiar. My eighth-grade teacher told me I would never be anything more than a janitor.

In single-parent African American households, the fathers are typically the ones who leave, and, although my dad wasn't exactly father of the year, he was a constant in our lives, which I later came to see as a rarity. At the time, however, none of the seven of us kids ever felt lucky to be statistical anomalies. We didn't want a mother who abandoned us and a father who stayed around. We envied people who had moms and dads in the house. We also envied those who never had to worry about whether there'd be food on the table.

Although we never knew it until the U.S. Census Man came around, my family was poor. Even after the report was released, we denied reality. Never mind that our father had defaulted on the mortgage and lost our little piece of the American dream at 559 Cedarhurst, or that the seven of us McLemores had to move into his parents', our grandparents', house (where we stayed until the day I went off to college), we didn't see ourselves as welfare-worthy. We didn't see ourselves as the N-word either. What we did see was a world in which everything that was good was classified "white" and everything that was wrong with the world was painted by prejudice and described as "black."

Those who were supposed to uplift us through encouragement and education judged us instead. As I look back at the moment my teacher prophesized what she saw as my inevitable future, I smell her stale coffee breath and my fists ball up involuntarily. To say I was angry would be putting it mildly. Her words put an exclamation point on my resolve never to live down to others' expectations.

Pops used to say "Life rewards action, your action will either make your life, or action will cost you your life"

Pops had a brilliant mind and a lot of wisdom to impart. Unfortunately, I had ADD/ADHD – although they didn't call it that then. There was Special ED, but in order to qualify for separated classes, or extra academic help, you had to have an obvious limitation. As far as anybody knew, I was inattentive. Whenever Pops launched into one of his little speeches, I'd get bored and wander off or find myself daydreaming too much to internalize all of what he was saying. If I had, I'd never have taken a pocketknife to two of my teacher's car tires. In my mind, she deserved it. I'd show her I could be more than just a janitor. I could be a vandal…

Letting my anger lead me stopped me from realizing what I'd later come to see as obvious – proving her wrong would have been much more satisfying than getting even in an underhanded way. I didn't just get even. I got caught with the knife in hand.

As my reward for my tire-slashing retribution, the principal expelled me and the cops gave me a free ride home. On the way from the school to my grandparents' door, the officers chided me for my bad behavior, but Dayton's finests' lectures were nothing compared to my grandparents'. When the officers left and Pops and I were alone, my grandfather ordered me to strip down to my shorts then took off his belt and let me have it, after which he banished me to my room.

"That's nothing!" he shouted as I dragged my sore butt upstairs to the attic bedroom I shared with my brothers. "Wait until your father gets home!"

I wasn't about to wait for my dad. I excused myself to go to the bathroom where I crawled out of the tiny window where, to my surprise, I collided with my unsuspecting father. Dad had been walking up the steps of the house at the precise moment when I scrambled out the window.

"Where do you think you're going?" he asked.

Caught in the act of escape, I had no choice but to follow him inside. I often wonder what would have happened if I'd stayed around longer, or daydreamed less, all those times my grandfather freely shared his wisdom. If I had paid more attention, would I have still chosen to poke my teacher's tires with a pocketknife? I like to think I'd have come up with a better plan.

Pops always said life either punished you for doing what you shouldn't be doing, or rewarded you, and held you up as an example, for doing what was right. Yet another of his lessons I didn't internalize until after I started playing high school football.

Long before I got into the eighth grade, I started doing the wrong things. I was angry with my parents for splitting up and, although I couldn't have articulated it at the time, I was acting out as a result of feeling abandoned and unloved.

Everyone loved my dad, Leroy. He was one of the best-looking men that ever walked this earth. He had it all – a great body, a smile that could light up Bourbon Street, and light brown eyes that would've humbled the great Billy Dee himself. It was no surprise that my mother would be so enamored with him that she'd give birth to four of his babies. She'd already had three of her own, all of which he accepted as his own. It was a good thing, too because, when she packed up and left town without notice, leaving all of us behind, Dad raised the seven of us the same. Not that that's saying much. He was more attentive to the bottle than his kids.

In my mind, I never felt wanted by either of my parents. My

mother escaped to California and even though my father lived with us, he wasn't, it felt like he was more absent than present. Still, instead of walking away when life got tough, he put us in a safe, clean, loving environment – his parents' house.

As much as I loved my grandparents, I longed for a two-parent, problem-free existence. I was naïve enough to believe there was such a thing. Now, I know that, if I sat in a room with 100 people, everybody in the room would have some version of a tragic story.

I was a child who felt abandoned by his parents, but that didn't mean my pain was worse than anybody else's. I don't have to look any farther back than my ancestors for examples of those who had it worse.

My ancestral history began on the lower deck of a boat that my ancestors had to row themselves. Even though they were heading away from home toward a place that promised only punishment and pain, they rowed. If they refused, they'd have been beaten to death and their bodies would've been tossed in the sea as shark bait. They arrived in a new and unfamiliar world only to be separated from their loved ones, beaten, chained and sold on auction blocks along with the pigs (and the pigs boasted higher prices). Even after they were set "free," because of Jim Crow segregation laws, there were still policies that restricted what they could and couldn't do.

Some might argue that I was born behind the eight ball, yet I've come to believe that when our mother left us and our father skirted his responsibilities by escaping into the bottle and pawning us off on his parents, my parents were introducing the seven of us kids to what I now define as "The System." "The System" is the not so secret secret to life. We can either make it work for us or against us.

My father seemed content with his role within the system, but I didn't want to go on record as being another black child living in what folks called a broken home. I lived out my entire childhood telling anyone and everyone that the reason my brothers and sisters and I were living with our grandparents was because our mother had died. Back then, no one was presumptuous enough to ask for details, so I was able to successfully lie to those around me without worrying about getting tripped up on the particulars.

The more times I told someone she had died, the more dead she became in my mind. Even though I said, and a part of me actually believed, that my mother was "dead to me," my heart ached. Somewhere deep within my gut, I thought I wasn't lovable enough for her to stay.

I was lucky though. I had people that were always there for me, with plenty of life's wisdom, insights, and love. My grandmother was the rock for the whole entire McLemore clan. She was the nucleus. I called her Mom and everyone else called her Mamma Annie. My grandfather, Joe Phillips and my late Uncle Bill were my first lifeguards. They provided a foundation I have come to appreciate, although I once took it, and them, for granted. They told me I was no trust fund baby and that the only way to get by in life would be to study "The System," then to work with it, rather than against it.

I was a sucker, they said, if I thought I could do something tomorrow. Tomorrow wasn't here yet, and yesterday was a history lesson that, once learned, would be easily forgotten. It was what I did with my time right now that defined who I was and what impact I would have on the people around me.

I listened to their stories of how far they had to walk to school in their day, with holes in their shoes, no hats, coats, and nothing but a nickel in their pocket for a peanut butter sandwich and milk, which they would trade for a sandwich made from hobo meat (bologna). But I didn't always pay attention. More often than I care to admit, Pops' and Uncle Bill's words bounced off the walls in my head. They had purpose. They were determined that nothing was going to stand in the way of what was rightfully theirs in life. And they were intent on imparting all their hardwon knowledge to me. Unfortunately, I was too shut down to absorb all the brilliance they were attempting to convey. Fortunately, despite my inattentiveness, some of their messages filtered through.

Uncle Bill was like a father/big brother/best friend all rolled into one. Pops was like a big rock in the middle of a super highway, secure in his place, daring anyone to move him, not caring if his presence was an inconvenience. I was a little afraid of him. I wasn't afraid of Uncle Bill. He could read me like a brand-new Marvel Comic book. He knew my pain without my ever uttering a word. It wasn't just me either. He claimed anyone could read what was in another man's heart by reading his eyes.

One day, being the "smart ass" that I was, I asked him to look into my eyes and tell me what was in my heart.

(Warning: If you have an Uncle Bill or anyone like him in your life, don't ever ask this question if you're not prepared to hear the truth).

Uncle Bill's pale green eyes bore into my dark chocolate ones. His breath tickled my nose. I inhaled the scent of toothpaste and shaving cream.

"Before you ever begin to think of yourself as something great," he told me, "you must kill that demon that makes you second guess yourself. If you want others to respect you as a person, you must respect yourself first. Develop what's inside." He poked his finger into my chest. "This is where your character lives. What's inside there is an important part of 'The System' of life. Make peace with what's in there and everything else will begin to fall into place."

At the time, I lacked the capacity to understand what he was telling me. I was convinced I had all the answers and that no one knew what I was going though. Now, at sixty, with the filters of youth, invincibility, false pride and self-righteous rage stripped away, I know that no truer words were ever spoken. Sometimes, when I'm feeling nostalgic, I'll raise a hand to my heart, place it where he touched me and understand that he knew the me I used to be better than I knew myself.

Pops was more insightful about life's principles and people than anyone I've ever met. He may've only been armed with an eighth-grade education (because he had to help raise and provide for his brother and sisters, he dropped out of school), but he read more books than people with doctoral degrees. He believed young folks should take advantage of every opportunity for a good education, both in the classroom and the world.

At 5'7", he walked with a deliberate purpose, head held high, and a self-confident look that said, I may not have a formal education, but I'm a well-read student of life.

The thing that I remember most about Pops is that he always had a book in his hands. Whenever a topic arose, whatever it was, he'd read a book about the subject and could therefore contribute to the conversation. It seemed as if his ability to read extended beyond the page. He'd be talking to me and looking up at the sky, as if he could decipher words written in the clouds.

Despite his ready access to information, he wanted to equip all seven of us grandkids with the skills to think for ourselves. So, in addition to his little lectures, he'd inspire us to arrive at our own answers. Once, he sat me down and asked me a series of questions:

Can people trust you to always do your best?

Are you sincerely committed to the task at hand?

Do you sincerely care about other people? If so, do your actions support that?

Do you have purpose? A reason to do something that will make life better for someone other than yourself?

Without waiting for my reply, he walked out of the living room, into the kitchen, sat down, and began drinking his coffee, leaving me to ponder over the seeds he'd sewn.

No matter how much Pops and Uncle Bill tried to enable me to question my motivations and evolve beyond my limitations, the streets called to me as loudly as the siren that warned everyone there was a storm coming.

I couldn't explain it, but it was a feeling in my gut that compelled me to use my sister's eyebrow pencil to draw a thin dark line above my lip and sideburns down the side of my face. I started hanging with the kind of fellas who never got an invitation to any parties but showed up anyway. I wasn't sure why they were so defiant, but I was filled with what I thought was justifiable rage and I felt at home surrounded by other angry outcasts.

It wasn't until the night these so-called friends and I were shot at by a gang that called themselves the Chains of Rap Brown (Dayton's version of the Crips and Bloods) that I realized that the road I was on was leading in one of two directions: a dead-end life with no meaning or purpose, or death. I should've known before that night, but I told myself I was entitled to do what I wanted. I ignored the nagging voice inside that sounded a lot like Pops when, during a conversation with my elder brother, Mac "Leroy Jr" and me, he said, "If you stand on the right side of the law, you'll never have to worry about the law standing against you." It struck me as a nice thought, but even as a young black man, I'd already figured out that the law seemed to be more comfortable with its boot on my chest and its finger on the trigger than with me standing by its side.

Like any other black male youth, I learned early that there was white law and black law. Black law… I thought about Martin Luther King and all the atrocities we were seeing on the news. But my grandfather had blind faith in "The System." He wouldn't listen to anything anyone said against it.

"Don't try to defy 'The System,' Kevin," he told me. "No reason to make life harder for yourself than it has to be."

Hard. I wanted to be hard. Yet, as I tried to outrun a .38 being shot into the darkness, I could feel whatever toughness I thought I had running down the inside of my pants. It didn't even dawn on me to be self-conscious about peeing my pants. Not when I was running for my life.

My friend, Jason "Bully" Kirkland, was the first to leap over the fence of Westwood swimming pool. As usual, I was right on his heels.

Jason was the toughest guy in our neighborhood. He could whip anybody young or old. He was the "friend" that taught me how to steal liquor from my grandparents' house, that stood beside me, each of us taking turns being lookout while the other picked the lock on someone else's bike. He was also the "friend" that suggested we beat down the kid who'd beat down a member of our crew. I trusted Jason as much as I could trust anyone. He was my best friend and, when we got to high school, he would turn out to be one of the toughest kids on our football team. Any time we were on the verge of a serious situation, Jason was the one I looked to.

He ducked low and we slithered on our bellies into the adjacent women's bathroom, where we hid and hoped...

I can still smell the acrid odor of gun smoke and see pieces of metal and dust falling around us. With every pop that hit the wall, I could hear the bullets calling my name. "It's only a matter of time before I find you, Kevin McLemore," each one said. "When I do, you'll think twice about beating up another member of the Chains of Rap Brown."

It didn't matter that my friends and I had only been retaliating. (One of the Chains of Rap Brown gang had beaten and robbed one of our friends). This was a high-stakes game in which we'd inadvertently engaged. They'd shown their hand. We'd tried to call but, instead of seeing our bet, they were upping the ante.

Pops used to tell me that a good run was better than a bad stand. That night, I figured out what he meant.

"Stay down low," Jason hissed.

How much lower could I get? I was face down on the ground of the girls' bathroom floor. I used to complain whenever my grandmother came out on the porch and yelled for us to come in, to beat our eight o'clock curfew. Now, I prayed, "Grandma, please call me home. I want to come home."

I no longer cared what my friends thought. Not even Jason. I wanted to live more than I wanted his approval. I mustered up enough of whatever I hadn't dropped in my shorts, picked myself up off the bathroom floor, and jumped back over the Westwood fence. This time, Jason followed me. For once, instead of running toward trouble, I fled from it.

Jason wasn't far behind me, and not far behind him were the Chains of Rap Brown. Shots rang out. Bang! Bang! Bang! As I zigzagged my way across the Westwood football field, I could have sworn I felt a bullet whiz past my ear.

Even though I had taken a path that led me to a game of chance with the Chains of Rap Brown, that night, I learned two things: I wanted to live more than I wanted to die, and I was fast.

I made it home safely. Jason did, too.

Neither of us told our parents, or, in my case, grandparents, what had very nearly happened. We didn't talk about it at all, except to each other.

My dad used to say that, if he asked each of his children to run to the edge of a cliff to determine our fate, my brothers and sisters would run close to the edge, then stop and look over to see how far they stood to fall, whereas I would run as fast as I could and leap into the air, never once pausing to see what I was leaping into. I would jump blindly. He said I always knew I was going to land on my feet. I wasn't so sure. Often, I did land on my feet, but, even when I didn't, I knew I'd be okay. Life had been knocking me on butt since birth. I only had two choices: stay down or get up.

SPRINKLES

The True Spirit of Christmas

Published by P. K. McLemore

Chapter 1.

In the North Pole, vanilla ice cream scoops of snow dotted the ground, while tiny marshmallow flakes fell steadily from the sky. It was a deliciously magical place, where dreams and toys were gifts for the asking. On this particular night, just two days before Christmas, a fierce wind was blowing, sending the snow flying in all directions. All of Santa's helpers were tucked away indoors, awaiting the birth of the newest reindeer.

They sat by a fire in a well-lit cave, enjoying the warmth, and talking about the baby being born in the next room. Santa and Mrs. Claus were there, as were a small group of elves and several of the woodland animals. Suddenly they heard a cry and they all jumped up to greet Mrs. Prancer's new baby.

Entering the tiny bedroom, they saw Mrs. Prancer cuddling her newborn reindeer to her chest while Prancer looked on lovingly. A proud father, Prancer turned away, so they wouldn't see his tears. But Mrs. Claus reached out and turned him back around.

"Happy tears are always welcomed, my dear," she whispered. She kissed his cheek and said, "Now let's see the little one."

Mrs. Prancer loosened her arms a bit and Santa rushed up first. "It's a girl!" he exclaimed grandly. "A beautiful little girl."

Sprinkles was tiny, barely bigger than an elf. Her creamy chocolate skin was sprinkled with milky white polka dots.

Mrs. Prancer smiled. "We'll call her Sprinkles."

Just as Mrs. Prancer spoke, a light gust of snow swirled through the bedroom, showering Sprinkles' face. She opened her eyes, blinked, and slowly looked at the smiling crowd surrounding her. Her smile was radiant, gleaming brighter than the whitest snow. Everyone who looked at her felt their hearts fill with joy and love.

But Sprinkles' smile faded suddenly, she closed her eyes and became very still. Everyone gasped!

"What's wrong?" cried Prancer, "She's not moving!"

Mrs. Prancer gently nuzzled her baby, trying to soothe her awake, but nothing happened. Sprinkles was lying there still as death. Then Santa decided to try. He took Sprinkles in his arms and let his beard tickle her nose. Finally, he looked up, shaking his head sadly, and said, "She's a tiny one, she is. The first reindeer to be born this early." Santa looked away from Mrs. Prancer, who was crying, and instead, focused on his loyal friend Prancer. "I'm sorry, Prancer."

Prancer continued to stare at his baby, letting his wet reindeer tears fall slowly to the floor. By now everyone was crying, and the warm, salty tears were melting the snow-hardened floor of the bedroom.

Just then, the flames from the fire began to rise. And as everyone watched in amazement, one of the embers flew out of the fire, and danced slowly around the baby reindeer's small, still body. But this was no ordinary ember. It's China, the Princess of Dreams, born of Sprinkles' need, and infused with her sleepy powers.

China put her ear to Sprinkles' chest and heard the soft but steady beat. With a flourish, she reached into a little pouch and sprinkled golden flakes into Sprinkles' lifeless eyes.

"From this day on," whispered China softly, "you will be the heart and soul of all mankind, the very spirit of Christmas. Now wake, and spread your love and joy throughout the world."

When China finished, she flew back into the fire and as the flames settled down, Sprinkles opened her eyes and cried. The cry was a tiny one, but it sounded like a symphony to Sprinkles' parents and friends. Tears were replaced with smiles, and everyone clapped and danced. Their hearts once again were filled with love and joy.

Santa twirled around and proclaimed, "Blessed be! Such a tiny thing, look at those eyes so blue. They will fill the hearts and souls of all mankind with love and joy." Then he turned to Sprinkles and proclaimed, "Sprinkles, you indeed are the spirit of Christmas!"

The fire in the little cave burned brightly all night, as Sprinkles' friends rejoiced in the little reindeer and her miraculous recovery. They were sure that everyone in the world would be happier now that Sprinkles was born.